arabesque

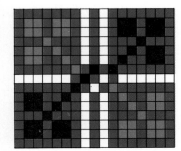

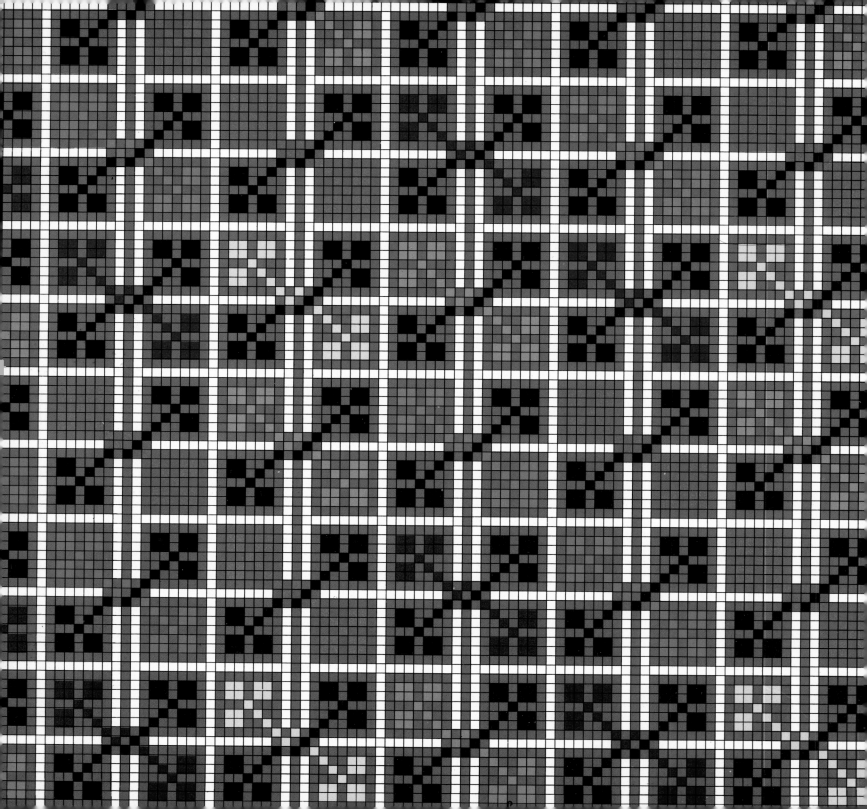

arabesque

decorative needlework from the holy land · ziva amir

VNR VAN NOSTRAND REINHOLD COMPANY

NEW YORK CINCINNATI TORONTO LONDON MELBOURNE

Designed by Magda Tsfaty
Photographs by Aliza Auerbach, Judy & Kenny, Benny Levanon

Graphic work done by Esther Frostig

Printed in Israel

Set by Otiot Dfuss, Ltd.

Published in 1977 by Van Nostrand Reinhold Company
A division of Litton Educational Publishing, Inc.
450 West 33td Street, New York, NY 10001, U.S.A.

Van Nostrand Reinhold Limited
1410 Birchmount Road, Scarborough, Ontario M1P 2E7,
Canada

Van Nostrand Reinhold Australia Pty. Limited
17 Queen Street, Mitcnam, Victoria 3132, Australia

Van Nostrand Reinhold Company Limited
Molly Millars Lane, Wokingham, Berkshire, England

16 15 14 13 12 11 10 9 8 7 6 5 4 3 2 1

Library of Congress Cataloging in Publication Data

Amir, Ziva, 1930-
  Arabesque.

1. Needlework — Patterns.   2.   Needlework — Israel.
3. Embroidery — Patterns.   4.   Embroidery — Israel.
I. Title.
TT753.A46   746.4'4   76-41849
ISBN 0-442-20290-3

contents

introduction

Them hath He filled with wisdom of heart to work all manner of workmanship, of the craftsman and of the skilful workman and of the weaver in colors, in blue and in purple, in scarlet and in fine linen, and of the weaver, even of them that do any workmanship and of those that devise skilful works. (Exodus 35:35)

The art of embroidery was well known and appreciated in biblical times. In this period it was confined to sacred and royal uses — garments, costumes, and accessories for high priests, the nobility, and the courts. Garments decorated with colored threads or gold wire, either woven or embroidered, were status symbols. They were made by professionals from expensive materials and consequently were far beyond the reach of the common man.

Alongside the art form, however, another kind of embroidery evolved. This was the folk art of the people, less sumptuous perhaps, but with a beauty and imagination quite its own. As needle and thread came into daily use, people used embroidery to creatively express their superstitions, beliefs, and traditions.

Embroidery from the Holy Land, like other crafts, preserved ancient motifs that have been passed down from generation to generation. The motifs reveal traces of the various empires and cultures that have flourished in this part of the world throughout the centuries.
Because cloth and threads are highly perishable, scarcely any work done prior to the last half of the nineteenth century exists. The embroidery ideas shown in this book date mainly from the end of the nineteenth century and later. The Holy Land was under Ottoman rule from the sixteenth to the twentieth centuries. At the end of World War I the British acquired a mandate for this area and brought with them many of the results of industrial change in Europe. The new materials and the European influence in general naturally influenced traditional styles and embroidery techniques.

Upper part of a back panel of a Hebron area dress

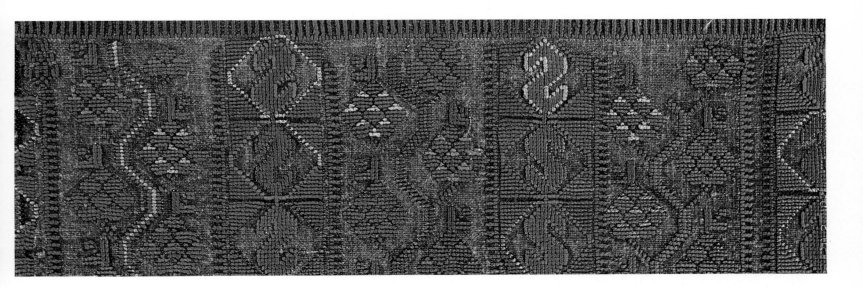

One of the strongest influences on folk art in this area was the Ottoman Empire. The Turks had inherited and assimilated into their culture many of the arts and crafts of the former Byzantine Empire. They had a highly developed textile industry, and their healthy commercial ties with the rest of the world helped the migration of textiles and embroidery motifs. This is why the same motifs are found in the Holy Land, in other Mediterranean countries, and even in more distant lands. Each country even each small region has added changes and embellishments of its own.

Until fairly recently Arab girls received no formal education. All their schooling was obtained within the home and the family circle. A girl was taught to work in the house and in the fields. Her work included fetching

A Bedouin woman in Sinai

water from the village well and grinding wheat for the daily bread. These duties took up much of her time. Modern technology has reached many of the Arab villages, making a woman's tasks somewhat lighter, but the routine remains more or less unchanged.

Embroidery was an inseparable part of a young woman's education. At about 12 years of age a girl begins to embroider and prepare her trousseau, or *kissweh* (which means "covering" in Arabic). She is guided and helped by the older female members of her family and by neighbors, from whom she copies designs while learning the rules and techniques of embroidery.

Small groups of women and girls sitting on their doorsteps chatting and embroidering are a familiar afternoon sight in an Arab village. In this way they spend what leisure time they have, taking advantage of the afternoon light and cool breeze.

Until her wedding day an Arab girl dresses very simply and modestly, with little embroidery or jewelry to adorn her clothes. All her attention is given to the wardrobe that she is preparing for her wedding day and for her future life as a married woman. A girl usually becomes engaged at about 16 years of age. With part of the dowry that her father receives from the bridegroom she buys the materials needed for her embroidery.

The materials customarily used were coarse, handwoven linens, either made locally or imported from Greece and later replaced by British machine-woven goods (generally dyed blue or black in the Gaza, Hebron, or Jerusalem workshops); cotton, either plain or striped with colored silk, from the town of Mejdal (near Ashkelon), which at one time was a well-known center for handwoven cotton; and small, narrow bundles of silk taffeta (about 7 to 8 inches wide) in red, green, or orange, imported from the famous textile centers of Beirut and Damascus. These materials and the small hanks of floss silk in rich shades of red and other colors, also from Damascus and Beirut, were all purchased in the nearest market town.

The kissweh A typical *kissweh* includes blankets, cushions, jewelry, and many embroidered objects — veils, headwear, jackets, and several dresses, both everyday and for special occasions. The number and type of garments differ from place to place, depending on local traditions and the prevailing fashion. A typical everyday dress is made of blue or black linen and has a modest amount of embroidery on the chest panel. The most important dress, the wedding dress, may also be made of a dark linen but is heavily and beautifully embroidered. Other best dresses from Beit Umar and the Hebron area in general are usually made of blue or black linen, while in other areas such as Ramallah (north of Jerusalem) unbleached cottons or linens are used. Festive dresses are also made from more expensive fabrics such as silk or a special black linen striped with colored silk. This fabric is used for the famous Bethlehem wedding dress (the Royal Dress).

The design of a traditional Arab dress is simple and easy to make. Most dresses have the same basic pattern. Modesty dictates that the dress be long enough to cover a woman's feet and wide and flowing enough to adapt

to changes in her body during pregnancy and with age. It basically resembles the ancient tunic, a fundamental prototype on which many folk costumes are based. The tunic, however, was usually made from one straight piece of fabric, with an opening for the head and neck and two straight pieces of fabric attached to it on both sides to form the sleeves. The Arab dress makes use of diagonally cut fabrics. Straight cut and pointed side panels are often added to the main body of the dress to allow freedom of movement. Triangular pieces of material are also added to the sleeves to form the winged, pointed shape so characteristic of the Arab dress. The sleeves are tied back when a woman is working.

The most outstanding example of this type of sleeve is found in the typical dress worn by the Bedouin women from Sinai. It has enormous pointed sleeves that reach to the ground. The sleeve is sometimes used for carrying small objects. This particular sleeve lends its name to the Bedouin *Abu Erdan* dress, which literally means "the father of the pointed sleeves." Dresses worn by the women of Gaza, by contrast, have narrow sleeves, as do the modern dresses from the Ramallah area.

The fabrics used for making an Arab dress are bought in rolls, which are cut in advance to the exact length needed. No material is wasted, and the valuable fabric is cut carefully in the right size and with the right number of pieces. Each piece is embroidered separately before the dress is sewn together, often in a decorative stitch done in colored silk. Dresses from each area can be identified by their fabric and cut, but the most distinguishing feature is the embroidery. The choice of colors, patterns, combinations, and

compositions make each dress style distinctive.

Decoration The chest panel contains the most important embroidery. The head, neck, and chest areas are considered to be the main life centers of the body. As in many old civilizations they are thought to be the most vulnerable and to need protection against evil spirits, the evil eye, and bad luck. Many means of protection are used: charms, talismans, beads and other kinds of jewels, and embroidery.

Embroidered chest decoration is found in many countries, but it is an intrinsic and essential part of every Arab dress from the simplest child's dress, with only a hint of embellishment, to the most elaborate. The Gaza dress and many Bedouin dresses have a huge V-shaped design at the chest area with very few patterns extending from it upward and downward. This design is embroidered directly on to the dress material. In most dresses the chest panel is embroidered separately and attached to the dress. An embroideress gives most of her attention to the chest panel. Some are exceptionally beautiful, covered with solid embroidery done in fine cross-stitches.

Second in importance to the chest panel is the lower-back panel. Its importance varies, depending on the type of dress and the region it comes from. In some villages dresses are decorated with a huge, carpetlike, solidly embroidered panel, composed primarily of very simple geometrical patterns. The back panel on a Ramallah dress is much smaller, and the patterns are arranged differently. The lower part is composed of the joined-

13

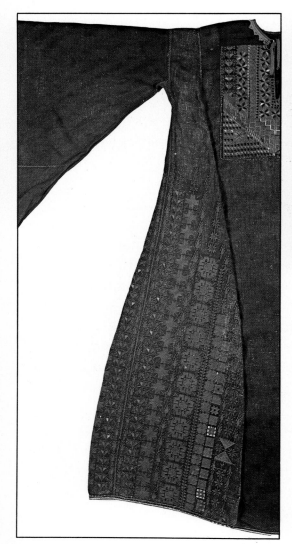

Side panel of Hebron area dress

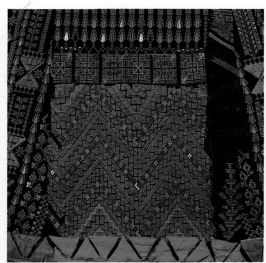

Back panel of Beit Umar dress

A Ramallah dress

Back panel of Ramallah dress ▼

chevron-palm-leaf pattern, one or two vertical border patterns, and a few horizontal patterns. Dresses from villages around Hebron are embroidered only in vertical border patterns. Everyday dresses have no embroidery at all on the back, while the lower back of the Royal wedding dress of Bethlehem is decorated in stripes of dark red, orange, and fine silver strands, which form the end of each roll of Royal fabric. Side panels completely covered with vertical rows of border patterns are typical of the Hebron-area villages. In other dresses, such as the Royal wedding dress, pointed silk panels in red and green are inserted at the sides and embroidered with cross-stitch and Bethlehem couching.

The classical Ramallah dress resembles the ancient tunic with its two embroidered decorative borders, which often consist of two or more border

15

patterns to create a richer look. This may have been the prototype for the dress style commonly worn today throughout the Judean Mountain region. The patterns used for modern Ramallah dresses are much more complex and elaborate; instead of combining two or three borders wider patterns are often chosen. Some are floral with animal figures, a strong European influence. The amount and type of decoration on the sleeves vary enormously from area to area.

Headgear It has been customary since biblical times for both men and women to cover their heads. The persistence of this tradition might be equally attributed to the religious concepts of modesty shared by Judaism and Islam and to practical reasons — to protect the body from the sun.

In modern times, with western influence and the elimination of religious restrictions, such customs are fading away. In the villages around the ancient city of Hebron, a Muslim religious center, however, the tradition is still strictly followed to the degree that a woman of the old generation would never show even the cap that she wears under her veil to a strange man.

Caps, bonnets, and hats vary from region to region but are often decorated with embroidery and adorned with coins, beads, and charms. Several types of veils and decorations are worn over the cap, the most beautifully embroidered of which are the wedding veils from the Ramallah and Hebron areas. These, like other wedding clothing, are worn later on festive occasions. Typical of the Hebron area is the huge linen veil combining three heavily embroidered small pieces — the head — and three long pieces

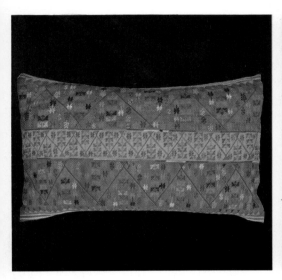
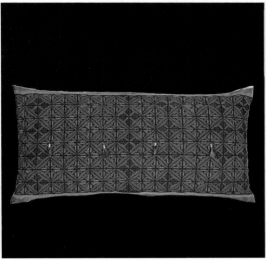
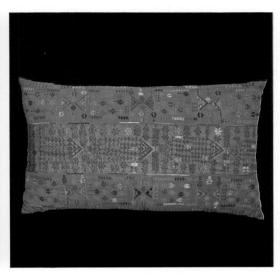

decorated with lighter embroidery. The classical Ramallah veil is smalle size and consists of only two linen pieces. Its two ends are richly embroidered with the joined-chevron-palm-leaf pattern distinctive to Ramallah.

Cushion covers and other embroidered items

Decorative wedding cushions are typical of the Hebron area. They are made for the young couple by their families. The bridegroom's mother embroiders the bride's cushion, while the bride's mother tries to compet embroidering the cushion for the bridegroom. These beautifully embroidered cushions are used by the couple during the seven days of wedding celebrations and then put into the chest along with the wedding dress and other treasured possessions. The most valued cushions are covered all over with solid silk embroidery that does not show the handwoven cotton cloth beneath; another type is made of the favorite ribbed silk with two red stripes at the sides and a central stripe in orange or green. As silk is a precious material, it is never covered by heavy embroidery but used as a background, forming an inseparable part of the pattern. Other items are embroidered by the bride as wedding presents to the bridegroom and his family, such as tobacco pouches, sashes, and caps.

Bethlehem embroidery Although the embroidery done by village or Bedouin women for their own use is a folk craft in the true sense, an entirely different style of embroidery flourished in Bethlehem and the neighboring villages of Beit Jallah and Beit Sahour. Bethlehem is at the same time a central market town for the surrounding villages and Bedouin tribes of the Judean desert and an important pilgrimage center for Christians from all over the world. It is well known for its local crafts. The especially rich Byzantine embroidey, done by professional embroideresses in gold threads or silk cords with floss silk, is much valued and highly priced all over the Judean Mountain region. The Royal wedding dress and short-sleeved velvet or broadcloth jacket, made to order by the embroideresses of the town, form an important part of the trousseau for women in the neighboring villages. According to local customs, in preparing for a wedding the family of the bridegroom used to go to Bethlehem to order the embroidered items from one of the agents in the town, taking with them a female relative of the bride as an advisor. Bringing the purchases to the home village was done with great ceremony.

*Upper front part of a Bethlehem
wedding dress*

Techniques and materials As most Arab folk embroidery was done on handwoven fabrics, counted-thread work was naturally the most suitable technique: the cross-stitch is the principal stitch used up to this day. It is usually made over two warp and two weft threads, so its size and shape are dictated by the weave, thickness, and evenness of the fabric. There are also striking examples of fine cross-stitch embroidery on ribbed silk, such as the cushion covers from the Hebron area. These are done freehand, often in light or scattered motifs. Freehand cross-stitch patterns are usually very simple, easy-to-follow geometrics. Freehand embroidery is still done by Bedouin women on black cotton-satin fabric, which is unsuitable for counting threads. Apart from the gold, silver and silk cords used for Bethlehem embroidery, done in the couching technique, all the embroidery was done in floss silk. Until it was recently replaced by mercerized-cotton threads, silk was used for embroidery all over the Near East and the Mediterranean. Although it is not the easiest material to work with, it is of incomparable beauty.

As fashions change, so do the materials. The use of mercerized-cotton threads, imported from Europe, for embroidery spread rapidly, along with machine-made textiles. Cotton satin and artificial silk satin and velvet, which are still the most popular fabrics, are not suitable for counting threads, so cross-stitch embroidery is usually done on a special canvas. The canvas is attached to the area to be embroidered, and, after the embroidery is finished, the canvas threads are pulled out one by one.

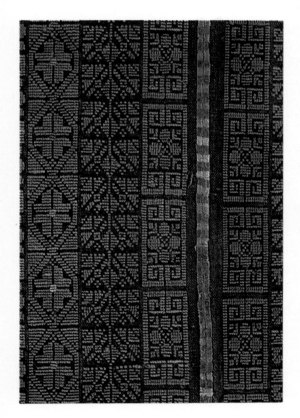

*Part of a side panel of
Bani Naim dress (Hebron area).*

The dominant color in Arab folk embroidery is red. Traditional silk embroidery was done primarily in a wide range of madder red from orange-red to brown; some was in a range of purple-red to purple. Red is considered a lucky color in the East and a protection against evil spirits. The madder plant was the principal red-dye source in the Holy Land in biblical times. Indigo-blue dye was produced from two plants, woad (*Isatis tinctoria*) and the true indigo plant. Blue is also a protective color; green symbolizes the Moslem paradise and is held sacred.

Motifs and patterns It is fascinating to watch an old woman in an Arab village read the familiar patterns on an embroidered dress as if it were a book. Some of these patterns have the same name in most regions, while others have more specific local names.

Although most of the names are derived from visual associations with the seemingly simple aspects of everyday life, their origins can often be traced to age-old cosmic or magical symbols. For example, the ancient idea of the tree of life is transmuted into a flowerpot. Among the fundamental motifs used until recently by Arab village women and still used by Bedouin women are the ancient symbols of the basic elements of nature — heaven, earth, stars, moon, sun, mountains, trees, and water. These symbols have been utilized since time immemorial to encourage the positive natural and supernatural forces that they are present. Just as a Christian woman might choose patterns with crosses, the Moslem woman sees a talisman in almost every triangular or diamond form and includes these in her repertory of patterns.

With modernization Arab villages have become less isolated, and the assimilation of city culture has inevitably caused the deterioration of many old traditions. Old materials and patterns have been replaced by new fashions; the carefully done folk embroidery has lost some of its originality and significance and been replaced by commercial machine-made embroidery.

The patterns shown in this book were selected from over 1,200 examples collected from Arab embroideresses of the Holy Land as part of a research program in this field. I have tried to choose the most classical, authentic, and typical traditional embroidery styles. Most of the patterns are shown as they are used in embroidered items. They all come from the central and southern regions of the country — from villages and Bedouin tribes where the folk craft of embroidery is still very much alive and the women are justly proud of it.

A beautiful piece of embroidery does not necessarily have to end up behind a piece of glass as a collector's item: it can decorate many everyday objects and add beauty to our lives. You will find the instructions in this book easy to follow, and hopefully you will feel inspired to try your hand at reproducing some of these lovely examples of folk art and to experience the satisfaction of the people who originally create them.

"Head" of a Hebron area veil

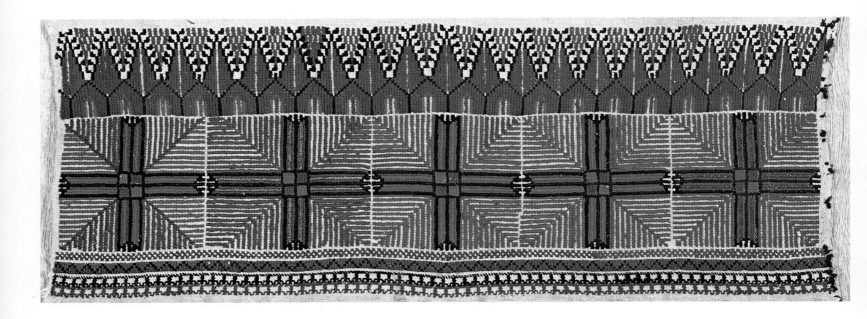

patterns

narrow and broad borders

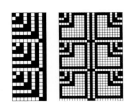

Borders are the principal type of patterns included in the wide repertory of Arab embroidery. In fact, most of the designs used in the Holy Land are border patterns in structure. The first three patterns (1-3) and their variations are used almost exclusively for framing; other border patterns are either used as vertical bands on the front and back of the dress or along the central line of the sleeve (as in the Ramallah dress) or arranged alongside other border patterns, vertically or horizontally, in order to cover an entire back or side panel of the dress (Ramallah, Beit Umar, and Bani Naim dresses) or the upper part of a chest panel (Beit Umar dress). As single, scattered motifs they appear on veils (as in the Dura veil) and silk cushion covers. Large patterns (9) are sometimes created by repeating the same narrow border.

The small selection of narrow-border patterns shown here, except for (5), is composed of the simplest motifs, toothed and feathered lines and triangles. Feathered patterns (1) are most common and appear in different sizes.

A smaller variation is shown on the chest panel of the Sinai Bedouin dress; a larger variation, on the back panel of the Ramallah dress. Feather motifs form a part of many tree, star, and quatrefoil patterns.

Toothed lines, or comb patterns, are considered to have a protective significance. The most common framing patterns are (2) and (3), while the combs on the cushion cover (4) and the squared combs and triangular pieces (6) are distinctive to the Hebron area. Another name given to these two patterns is Jewish tombs, from similar shapes observed in ancient Hebrew tombs. The leach (5) is one of the oldest textile motifs. It originated in the ancient Near East and spread all over the world. It represents the serpent, a symbol of life and health. Other narrow-border motifs are the key of Hebron (7), a ladder (8) and roses (9).

Some common geometrical broad borders are shown here. The simplest make use of the squared-palm-leaf (a form of feathers) motif (10 through 15), the comb motif (13 through 16), or a combination of both (13 through 15). Some are arranged symmetrically on both sides (10,11,16), while others have a quatrefoil form. Of these patterns only (11) has an exclusively upward direction; the rest can be used in any direction. Talismans and squared palms (10)

is a typical Sinai Bedouin pattern. The road to Damascus, or the road to Egypt (11,12), is given to many patterns composed of rows of the thick, squared-palm-leaf motif, arranged either in pairs or in small quatrefoils (12 appears on the Hebron veil). A square piece of soap (13,14) is another common motif, as are the officer's badge (15) and the comb (16).

These broad-border patterns are more complex. Most of them are constructed of rectangular units (17,18,19,21,22), some with an inner frame in a lozenge, hexagonal, or octagonal shape (17,18,19,20). None has a particular direction except for (23). Some (19 through 23) can also be used as geometrical floral borders. A black pattern (17) and a green pattern (20) are names describing the colors in which these designs used to be embroidered although no trace of green appears in (20). The leach pattern (18), with or without the comb frame, is even more common as a broad than as a narrow border all over the Judean Mountain region (as in the back panel of the Hebron dress). Other broad borders are the eye of the camel (19), a feathered pattern (21), and toffee sweets (22), all three of which appear on the side panel of the Bani Naim dress. A more recent pattern (23) is sometimes given the name of the Moslem holy city El Medina El Menawarah by women from the villages around Hebron.

chevron palm leaves

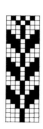

are the simplest and easiest motifs to embroider by counting threads. Variations of the two chevron single-leaf patterns are found everywhere in old-type embroideries, while the pattern in which they are joined together to form a solid body of embroidery (26) is distinctive to Ramallah. All three variations are called date palms; the single types (24,25) are also known as ears of corn.

cypress trees

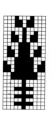

Although the cypress tree is not native to the Holy Land, it was well known and venerated in the ancient Near East. Its highly valued timber was imported from Tyre by King Solomon to build the temple in Jerusalem. It is one of the tree-of-life symbols, referring more to eternal than to earthly life, and is widely used in the arts and crafts of the Near Eastern countries. It is one of the principal motifs in Arab embroidery, found on almost

every old dress or veil either as a single unit or in vertical, horizontal, or diagonal rows as a component of another pattern. It forms an intrinsic part of most southern Bedouin and Hebron area talisman patterns (as in the Dura veil and the Bedouin dress). A combination of cypress trees and mountains is used on the head of Hebron veils; (27) is typical of Ramallah (a single unit on the chest panel of the Ramallah dress), while (33) is characteristic of the Gaza area.

trees and flowers

Also represent the tree-of-life idea, symbolizing growth and abundance. Every dress or veil has some growing pattern, either a palm or cypress tree or a floral pattern. A variety of tree and floral patterns is shown on the following pages, from the simplest Bedouin tree to the more sophisticated floral patterns, which reveal a European influence. The tree is usually an upward growing pattern, with a central stem line and symmetrical diagonal branches. Some of the motifs are a tree of triangular pieces (36); a squared date palm (37), one of the most common patterns and found in many variations (as in the silk cushion cover and the chest panel of the Beit Umar dress); pots

with date palms (38) and snails (40), seen on the side of the Beit Umar dress; and the loquat, or feather's tree (39), distinctive to the chest panel of the Ramallah dress.

Slanting flowers are often seen in embroideries from Turkey, Greece, the Balkan states, and North Africa. They are also widely used in the Ramallah area, where they are known as half-opened buds, date palms (43), or feathers (44). A tree (41) the simplest of these patterns, is typical of Hebron work.

The half-opened buds of the ten (42,44) refers to the width, which consists of ten stitches with (4) or without (2) the stem line. If the width is doubled (43, 45,46), the pattern is called the tree of the half-opened bud or the big half-opened bud (46,47).

The last four patterns in this group are more complex. While the first seems to be an elaboration of the local tree idea, the others show distinctive western influence.

grapes

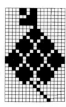

Vine branches with grape clusters have been one of the favorite themes in the arts and crafts of the Holy Land since ancient times. One of the many variations common in the Judean Mountains (52), a region famous for its vineyards since biblical times, is called grape clusters, snake grapes, or camel footsteps. A doubled variation is shown in (53).

rosettes

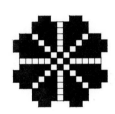

The rosette is one of the oldest motifs found in the textile arts. It seems to have spread from the ancient Near East to Europe, where it is found in folk cross-stitch embroideries of many countries. It was most popular in old-type embroidery done in this country especially as a border pattern (55,56). The classical rounded-petal rosette (54,57) and the toothed-petal type (55), framed and arranged either in a vertical row or in a solid block, are characteristic of Ramallah and are still used in commercial embroidery. The stemmed type (56) is typical of the Hebron area. Both (54) and (56) are called flowers; (56) is also called the bottom of the coffee cup; (55) is known as the cow's eye or foreign moon; (57), as moon of roses.

stars

Of all sacred symbols of heavenly elements worshipped by man since prehistoric times, the eight-pointed star of Bethlehem is perhaps the most common as a textile motif. It is used by Moslems as well as Christians. Stars with or even without a stem or leaves are often referred to as trees or flowers, especially in the Hebron area. A tree of eight (65) a strange tree or a rotating tree refers to the rotating effect created by changing the order of the colors inside the star sections. Some motifs are called stars; others are moons, such as the moon of Behtlehem (64) or the moon of doves. The six-pointed star (67) occurs as a border variation (as on the chest panel of the Ramallah dress) and as a single unit (the talisman pattern from the Hebron area).

quatrefoils

Quatrefoil patterns, either entirely feathered (68,70) or of the tent type (69,72), are characteristic of the heads of veils in the Hebron area but were also embroidered on the back and side of dresses. Their cruciform structure probably appealed to the Christian women of Ramallah, who displayed single-unit patterns of this type (71) in a prominent location (symmetrically arranged on the classical chest panel of the Ramallah dress). They also used these patterns in rows to form vertical or horizontal bands. Among the motifs are the star of feathers (68); the tent, or tent of the Pasha (69,72); the tree of sticks (70); and the feathered moon, a typical Ramallah design.

talismans

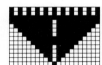

The Arabic name *hijab*, which means "talisman," is given to many triangular-shaped patterns. The triangle is the most important basic motif in traditional embroidery of the Holy Land. Some typical talisman patterns in which the triangle is doubled and repeated in different ways are shown here. In most cases they are called talismans or double talismans, but some have other names as well, such as (73), from the Hebron area, which is also called apples or flowers, and (75), which comes from Ramallah and is known as kohl bottle or flower pot. Motifs (73,74,77,78) are from the Hebron area; (76) is a typical southern Bedouin double talisman with cypress trees. Another talisman pattern with a pair of birds is shown at the end of this chapter.

diamonds

The first three patterns, which are older than the rest, bear a strong relationship to the talisman patterns — multiplied or doubled triangles forming diamond shapes. (79) is a characteristic Sinai Bedouin pattern; (81) distinctive to the Hebron area, is called square talisman. Patterns (82 to 86) are distinctive to the Ramallah area and were introduced from the west sometime after the beginning of this century. They first became popular among Christian women. The accent on the cross shape suited their religious feelings, while the basic straight and diagonal lines made them ideal for filling the triangular lower corners of the chest panel. This fashion increased in popularity and spread to the surrounding villages, Christian and Moslem alike. The motifs have the following names: (82,83) sweets and sugar on a plate, (84,85) the corner of two and one, and (86) the corner of the cow's eye, still one of the most popular chest-panel corner patterns. The two

diamond patterns (87,88) represent a special group of complex, single-unit patterns is always accented, often the diagonal cross (St. Andrew's cross) as well. The moon-of-stars motif (87) is composed of traditional patterns, while the moon of the half-opened-bud (88) shows European influence. Moon patterns used in the center of the chest panel have a clear diamond-shaped outline (88), while those located at the lower corners (87) are squared.

flowerpots and birds

Birds are generally considered heavenly messengers, symbolizing the human soul and spirituality. The dove represents the Holy Spirit in Christianity (93,94) and is a universal symbol of peace and love. Birds are often associated with the tree-of-life motif or its later derivatives, the flowerpot or vase, a common theme in folk embroidery all over the world. The cock (92) is the emblem of sun, glory, and male virility. The Moslems believe that it drives away darkness and evil spirits and calls the believers to prayer. Birds (89) and a branch of birds (91) are variations of the same motif, which can be used as a single unit and as a continuous overall pattern based on the tree of life, since they

include the potted-tree element. A single bird is shown in (95,96). The flowerpot (90,97) is distinctive to Ramallah; (90) is the more common; (97) is also called pattern of the railroad because of its resemblance to tracks. Design (98) is called potted fruit-bearing tree with birds on flowers. The two patterns on the front cover are cypress trees with combs and mountains in the upper row and tents of the Pasha in the lower row.

Part of a side panel of Bani Naim dress (Hebron area). ▶

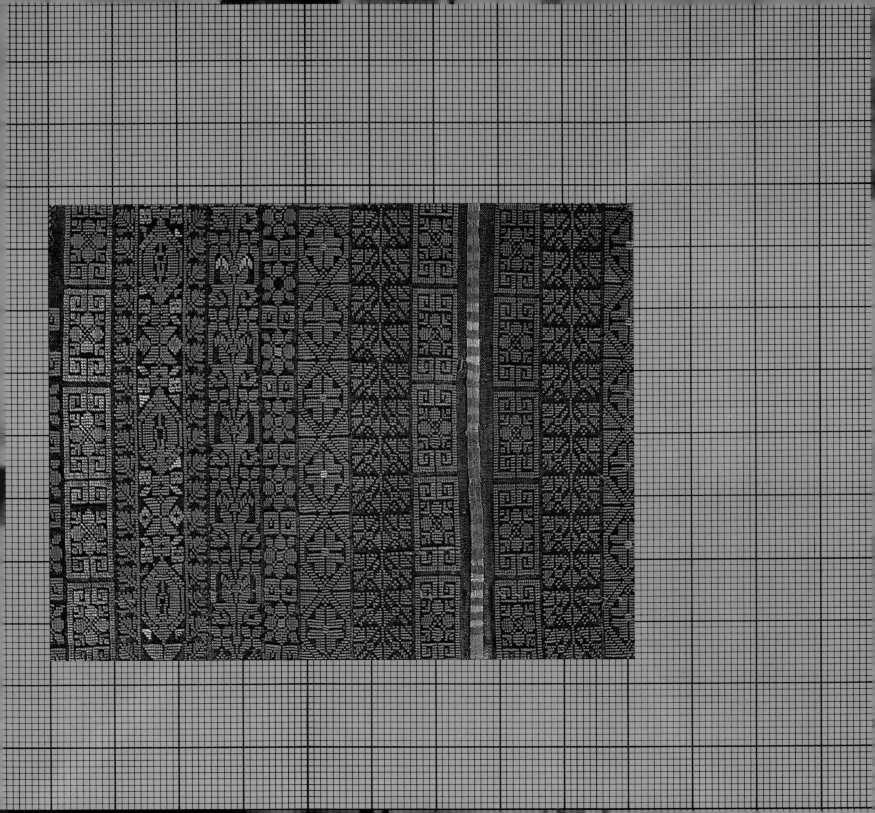

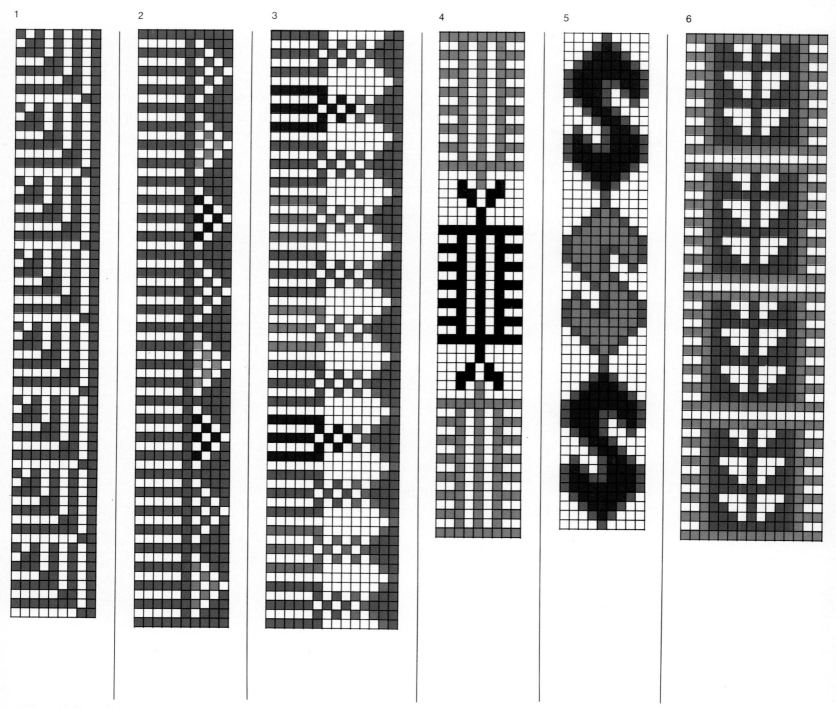

narrow borders

7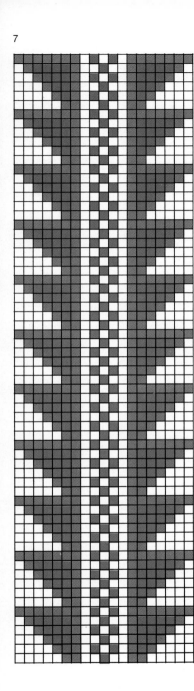

8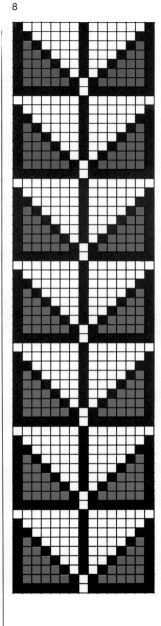

9

29

10

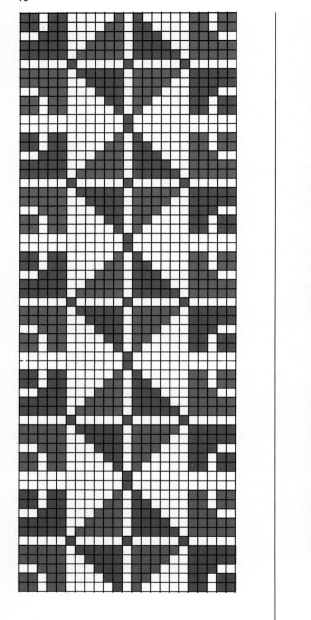

11

12

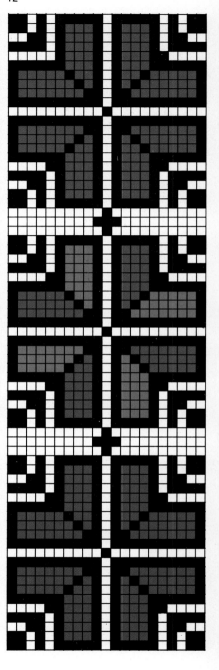

broad borders

13

14

15

16

17   18   19

20   21   22   23

24 25 26

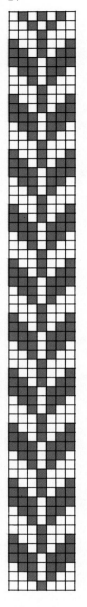

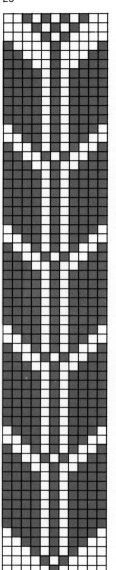

chevron palm leaves

28

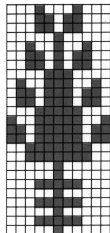

29

30

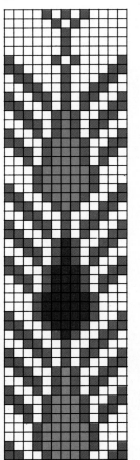

31

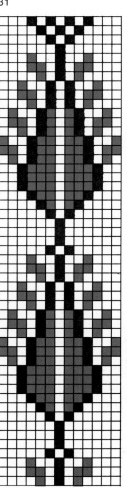

32

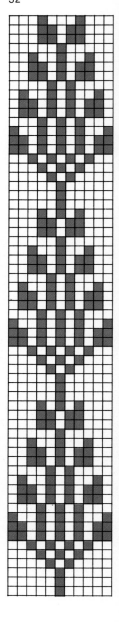

cypress trees

34

33

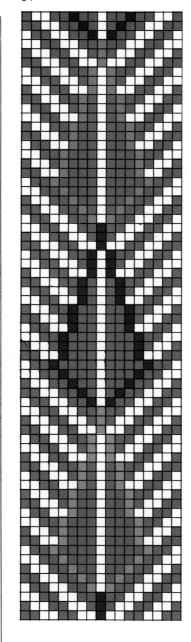

35

trees and flowers

41

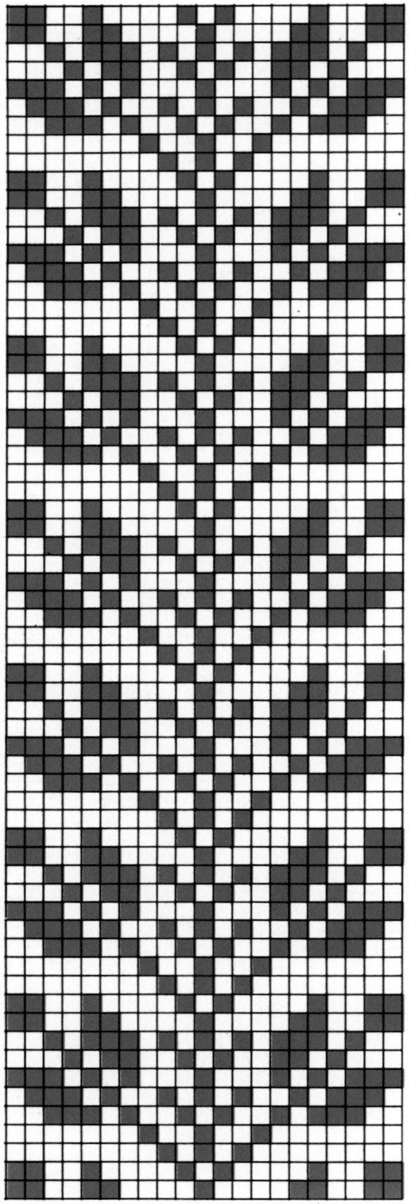

42

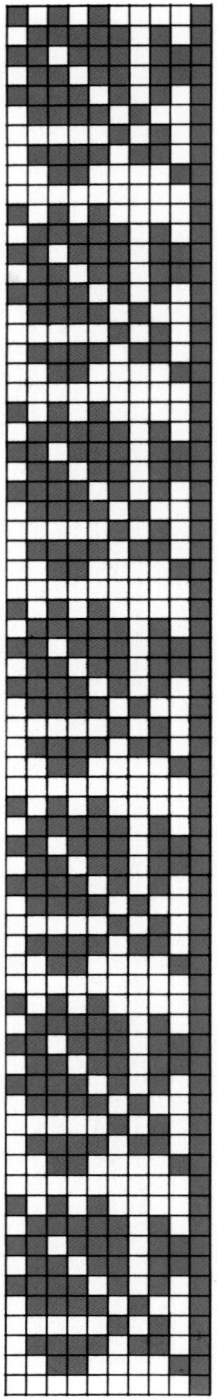

43

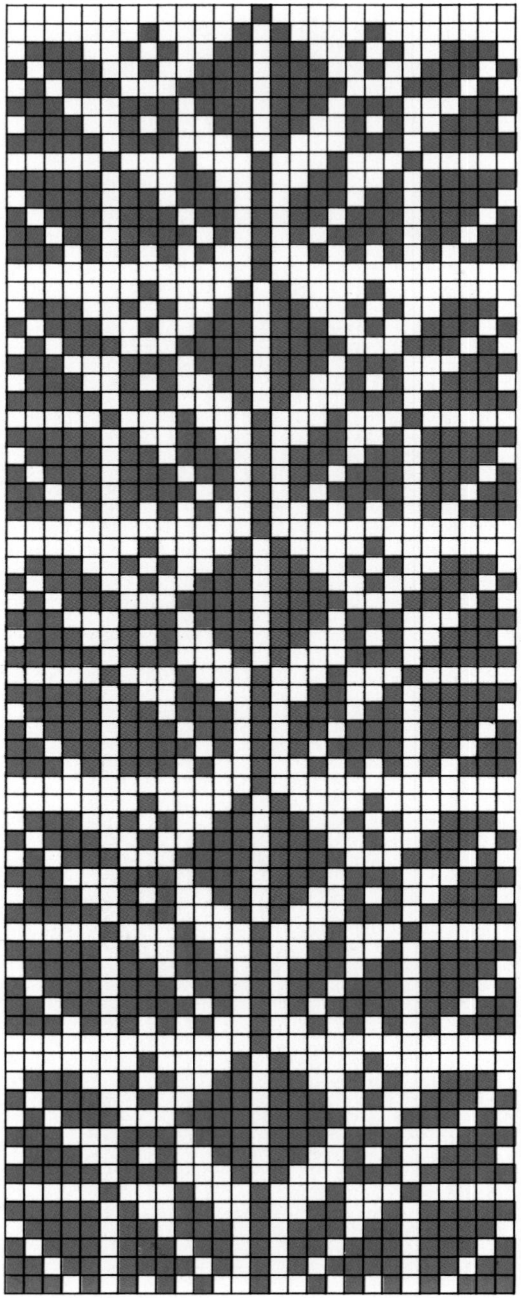

44

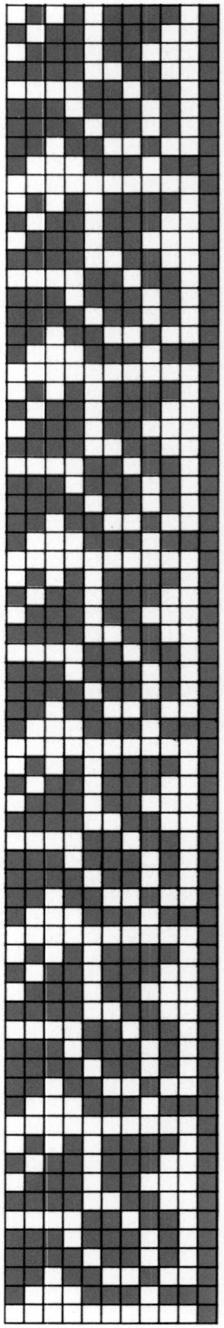

45

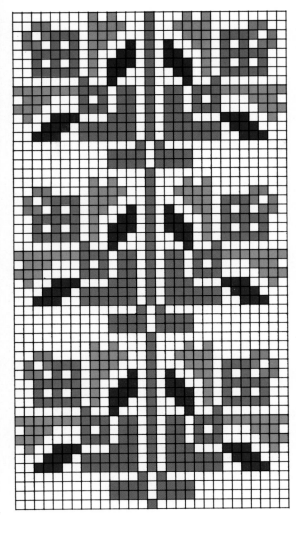

46

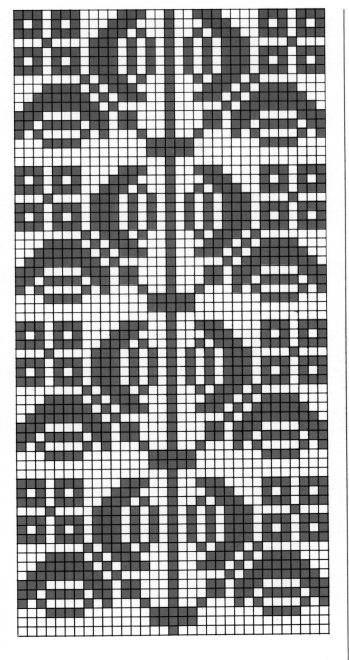

47

48

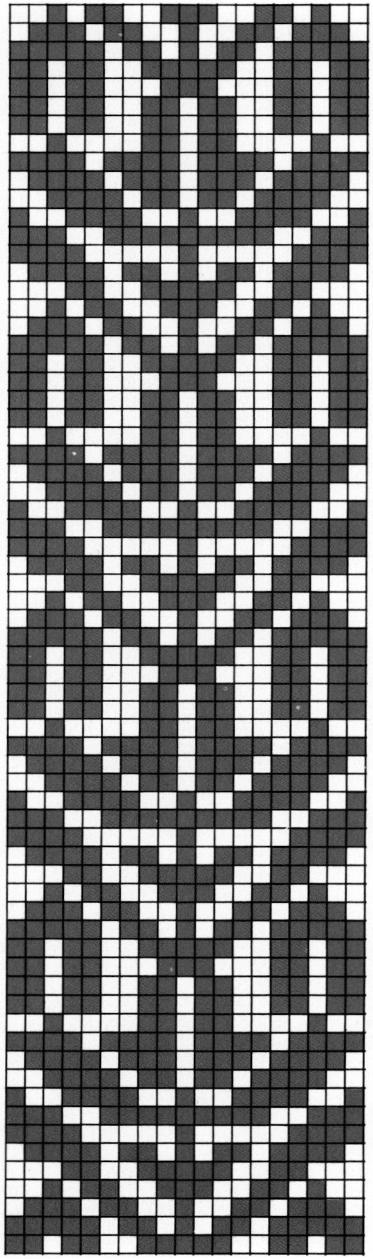

49

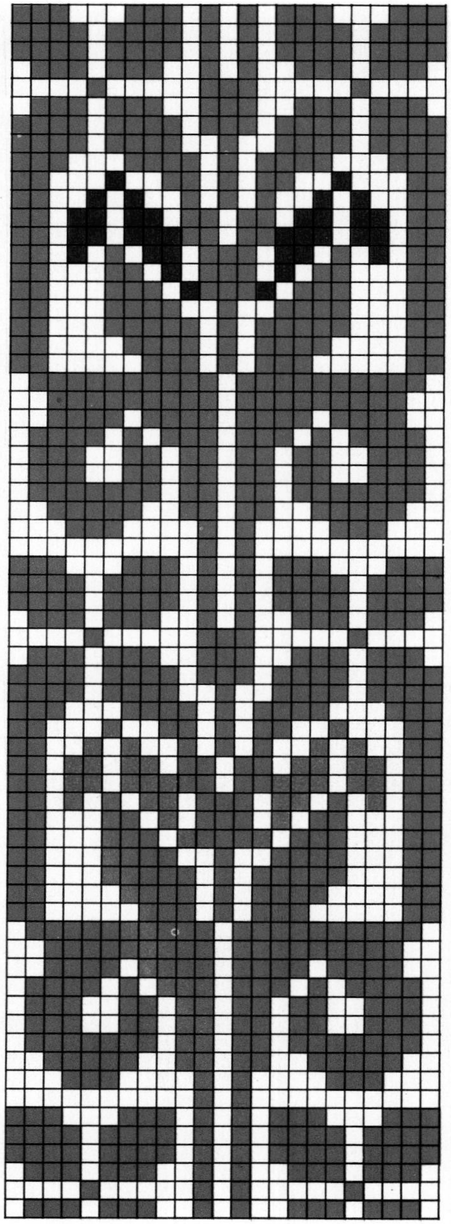

50

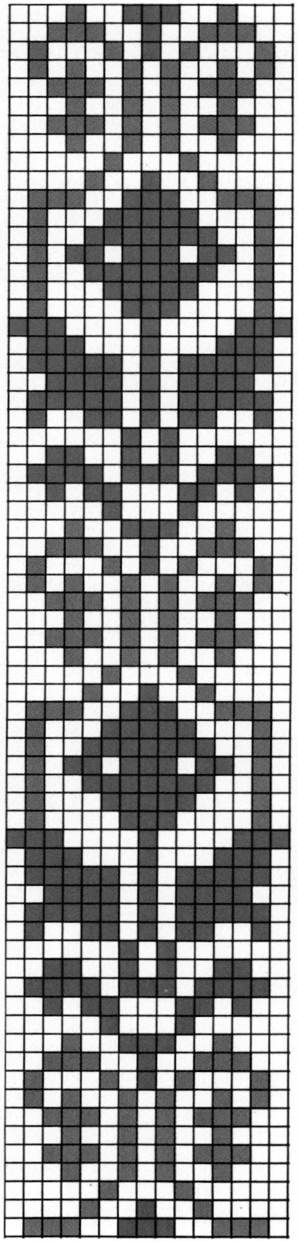

51

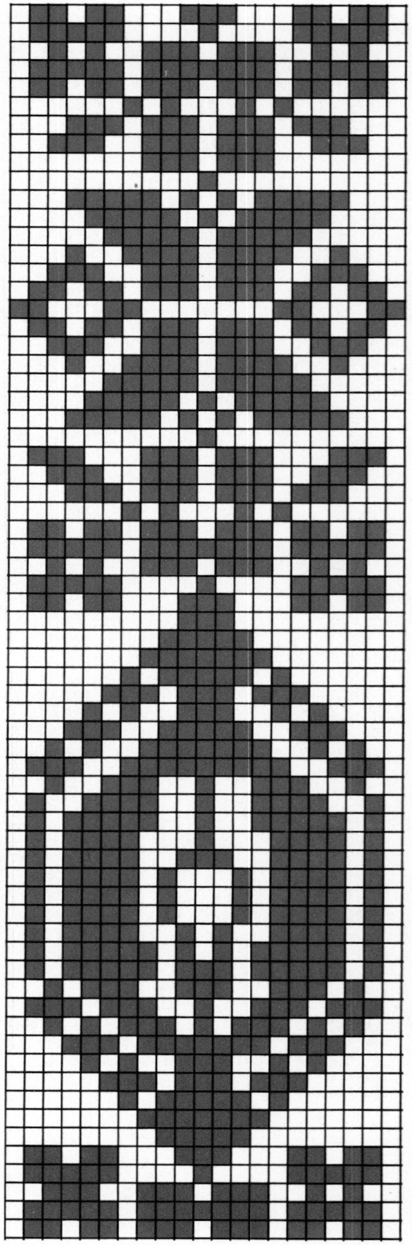

grapes

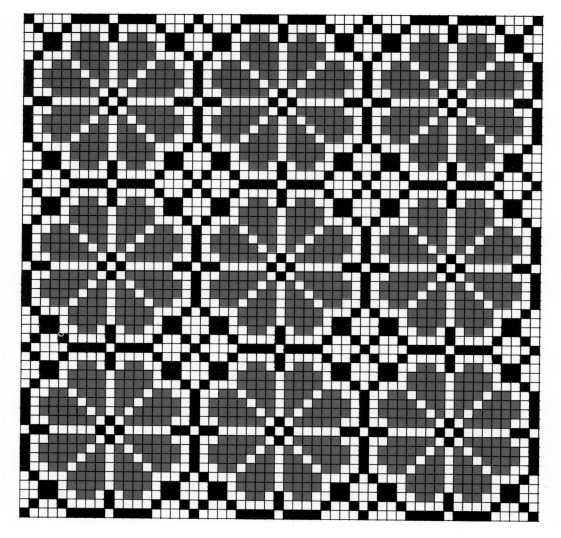

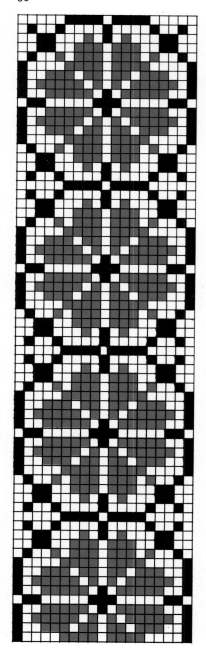

rosettes

58

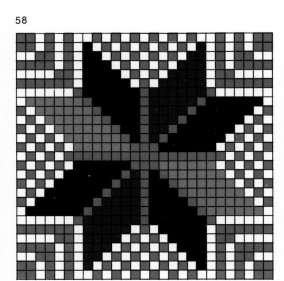

59

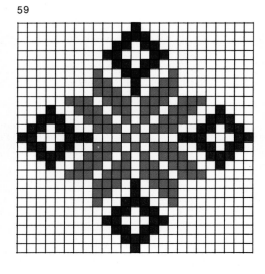

60

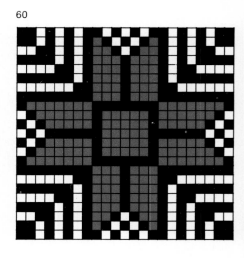

61

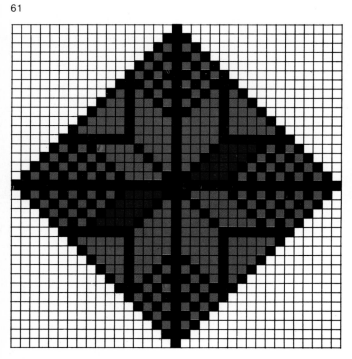

62

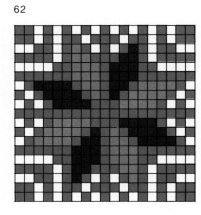

63

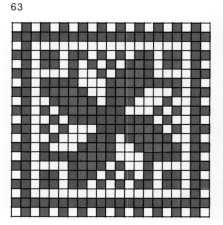

stars

64

65

66

67

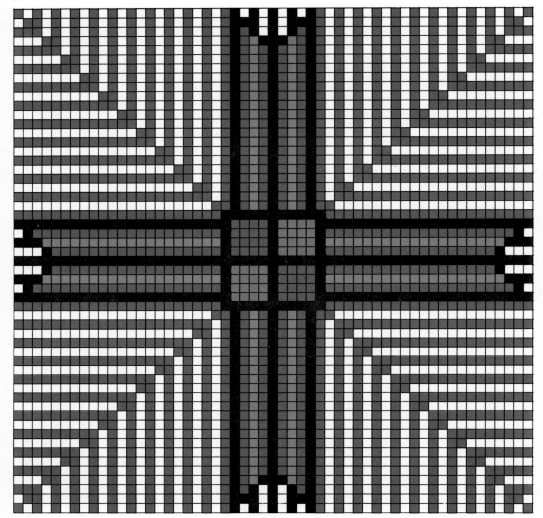

quatrefoils

48

69

70

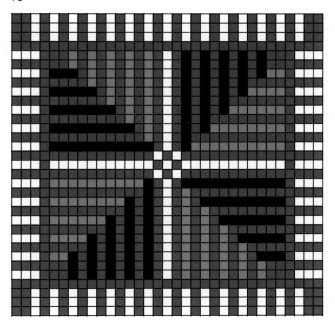

71

72

74

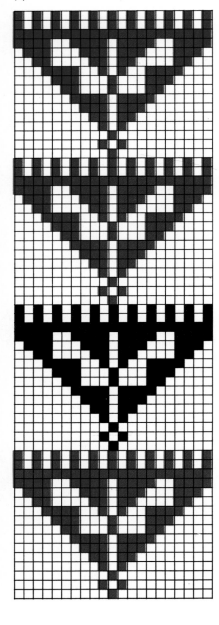

73

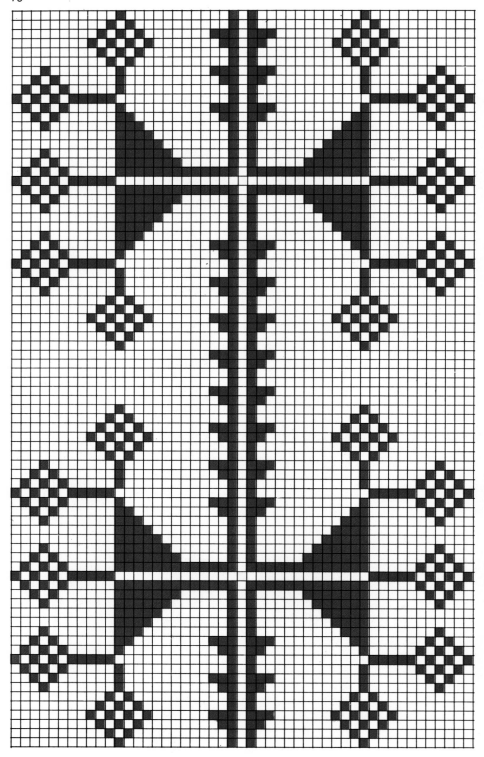

talismans

50

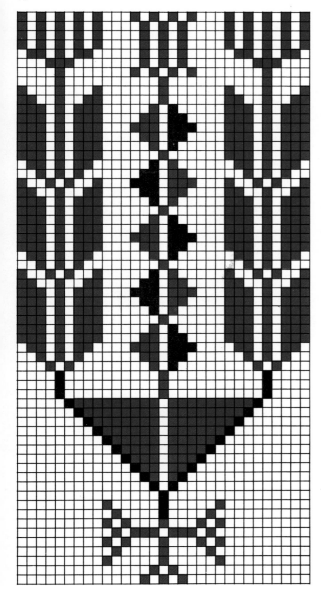

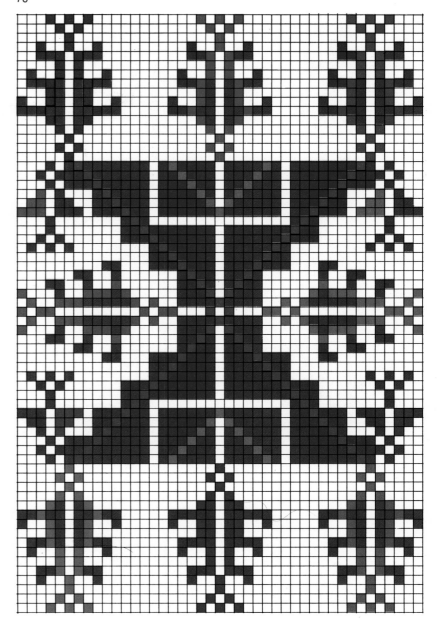

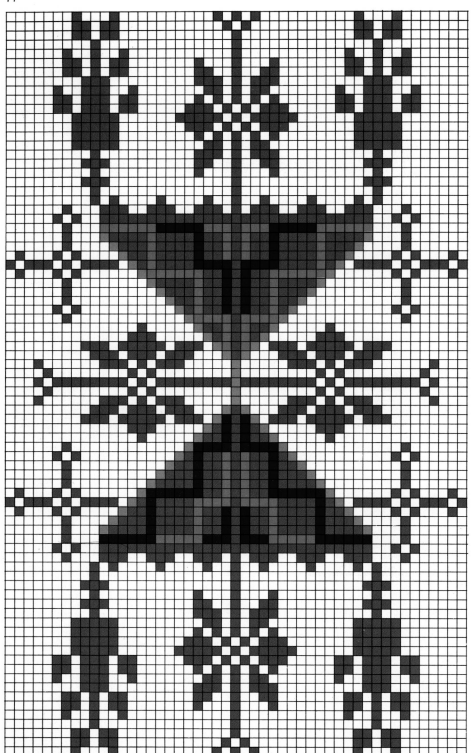

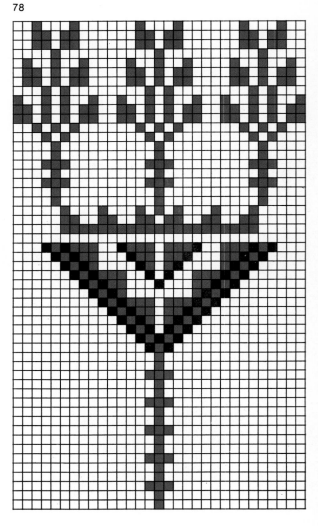

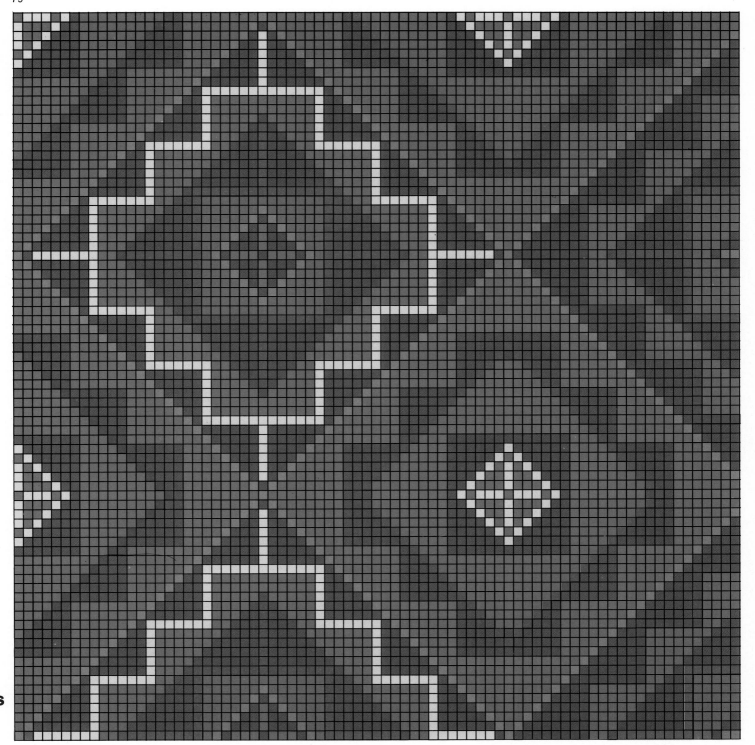

diamonds

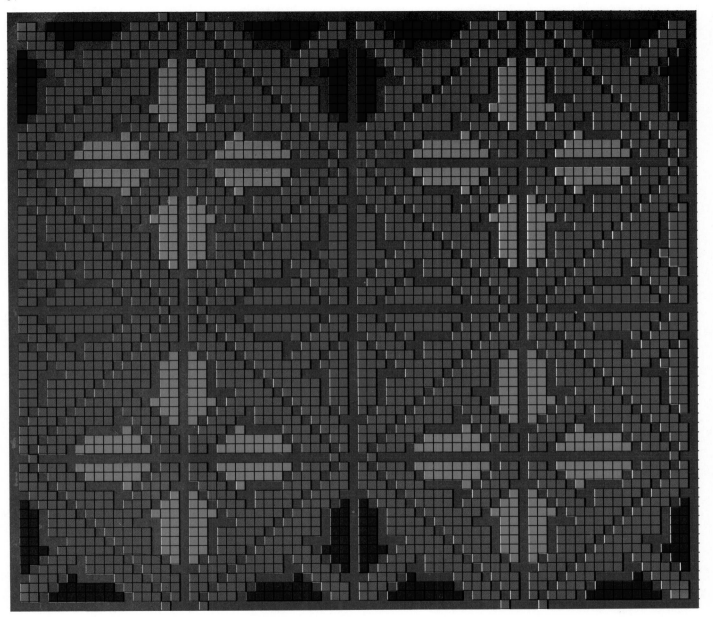

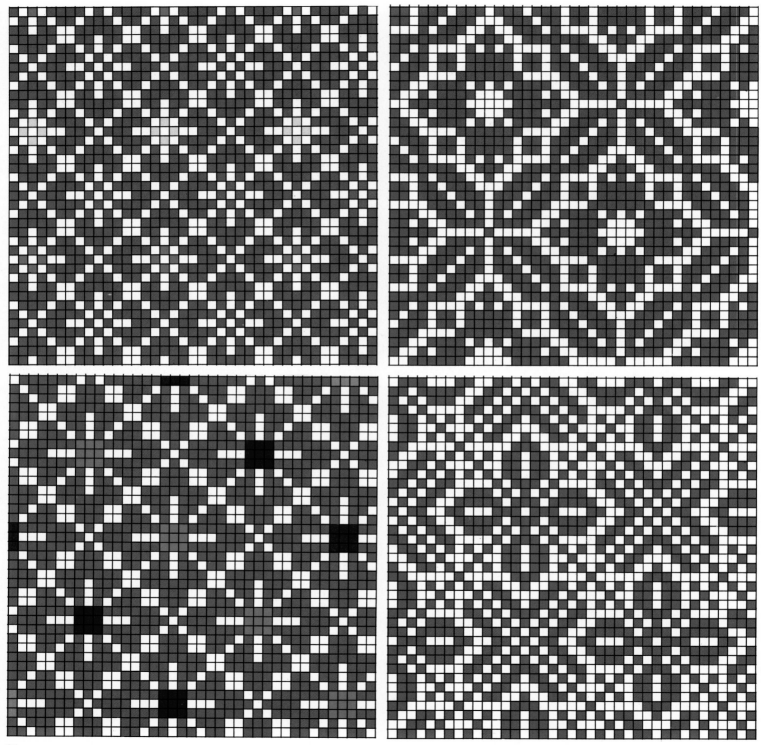

82

83

84

85

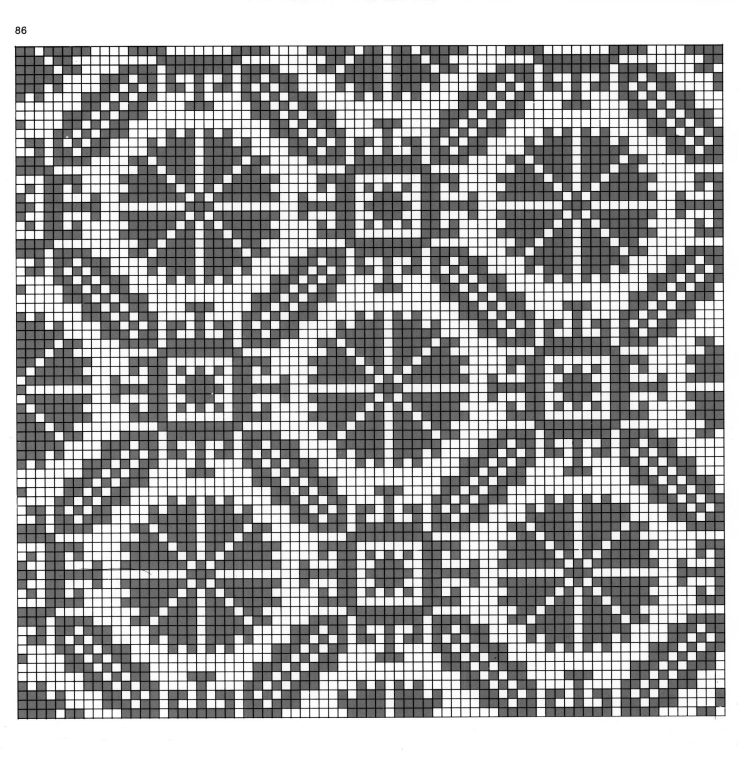

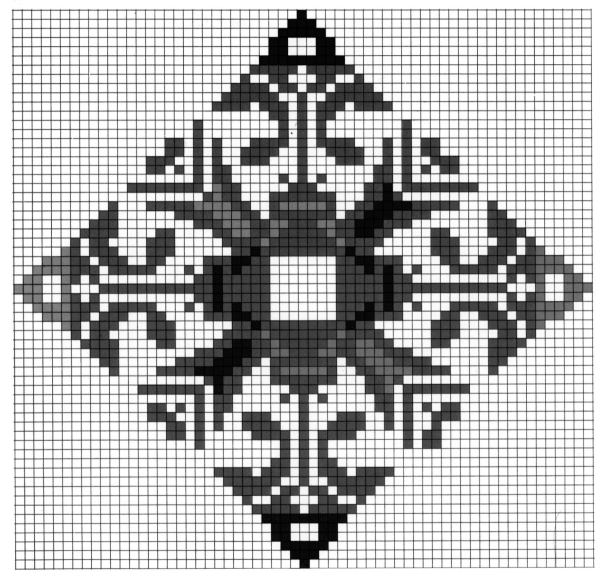

89

90

91

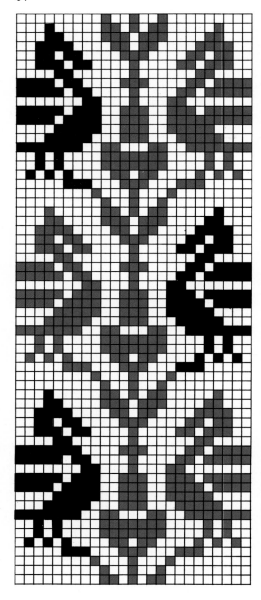

flowerpots and birds

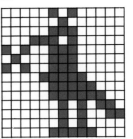

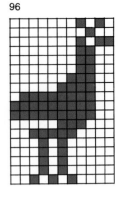

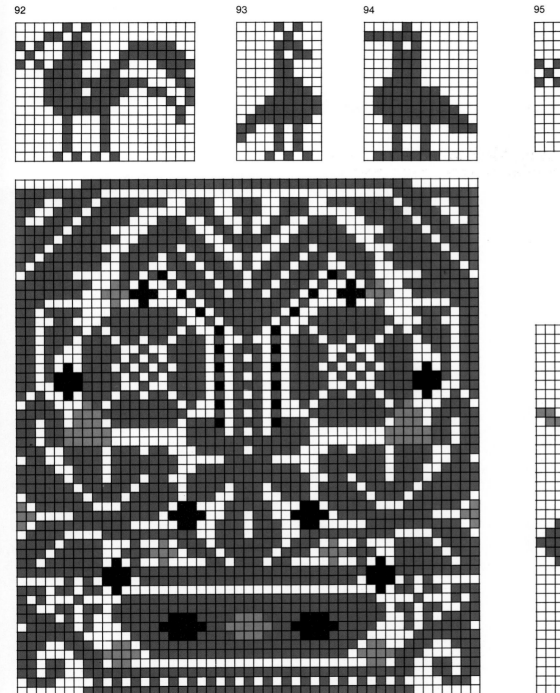

97

98

instructions

fabric and needle

The ideal fabrics for cross-stitch and other types of counted-thread embroidery are even-weave fabrics in which you can see and count the threads easily — linen, jute, cotton, or wool are ideal. Open-textured, coarser materials are generally easier to work with. You will find that soft wool or cotton materials are more suitable for clothing, while stiffer fabrics such as linen or jute are best for tablecloths, bags, cushions, and book covers. A round-pointed tapestry needle is used with these.

If you use a fine fabric in which the threads cannot be counted — silk, for example — you will need special embroidery canvas. It is attached to the area to be embroidered and removed thread by thread when the embroidery is completed. This canvas is sold in embroidery stores in different densities to suit the size of the cross-stitch. Fine fabrics are suitable for more delicate clothing items such as blouses or dresses. This kind of cross-stitch embroidery is done with a sharp-pointed (crewel) needle.

threads

It is very important to match the thread to the material. For fine fabrics stranded cotton in groups of two, three or four strands is advised, while for thicker fabrics either groups of four or six cotton strands or pearl cotton embroidery threads, size 8, are used.

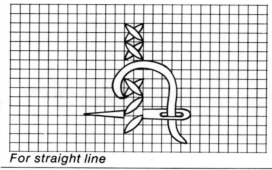

For straight line

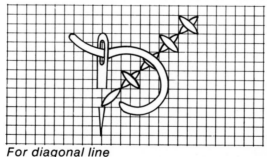

For diagonal line

draft

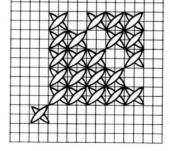

the embroidery

The draft and it's actual outcome

Size 5 pearl cotton is suitable for coarser fabrics and large cross-stitch. Tapestry wool is used to embroider woolen clothing items, cushion cover, bags, and wall hangings.

colors

The illustrations in this book show the authentic colors of Arab embroidery. Unbleached linen or cotton in off-white, indigo blue, and black predominates as backgrounds. Shades of crimson, orange, and green — typical colors for embroidered silk cushion covers — can also be used. You may use different combinations of colors. To choose a pattern, look at each one separately. Study its character, its direction and its shape.

patterns

Some pattern suggestions are also given in the photographs, but there are almost endless possibilities. Apart from using the patterns given here, you can either form a row of single units, separate motifs in a row, or combine patterns. You can also double a motif by using a small mirror or even create a quatrefoil pattern.

measuring

To organize your work, start by measuring the area of the object that you want to embroider. Next measure the size of the pattern you have chosen and plan the position of the embroidery on the object. The size of the stitches depends on the density of the fabric. The best way to determine the number of stitches that can be made in your fabric is to sew a short, straight line (1 inch or 2 cm) in a contrasting color of running stitch the same size as the intended cross-stitches, counting either two or three threads of the fabric, depending on your chosen size of stitch. Find out the number of stitches you have per inch or cm, then count the number of squares in the pattern drawing (each square equals one cross-stitch).

If you want to embroider a single-unit pattern — on a tablecloth, for example — here is the best way to do it: cut some pieces of paper to the size of each unit, spread the fabric out flat, and play around with the pieces of paper until you find the design you want. Mark the place with a line of running stitch in a contrasting color.

If your embroidery is done on a canvas, it is a good idea to draw the design or its basic lines on it with a marker pen. (Don't forget to put white paper underneath the canvas to protect the table). You can draw the entire pattern on the canvas: it might seem like too much work at first, but it saves time and trouble later. Cut the canvas out, leaving a selvage around the exact size of the pattern. Attach the canvas to the fabric with running stitch, using a fine cotton thread.

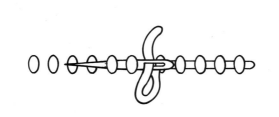

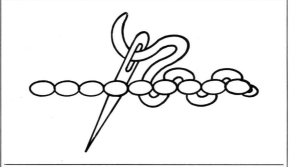

Three ways to finish the edges of the threads

cross-stitch technique

Each square in the illustration stands for a single cross- stitch, which is usually done over two warp and two weft threads of the fabric but may also be done over three or even four threads.

To obtain a smooth finish in your embroidery, the upper arms of all the cross-stitches should be kept in the same direction. Plan your embroidery route first in order to keep the reverse side as neat as possible.

Both ends of the embroidery threads should be inserted through the stitches formed on the left side of the embroidery for about 1 inch, depending on the size of the stitch.

To start a new thread, allow for extra length, which can be tucked in for a neater finish. Never leave long, loose threads hanging on the reverse side of your embroidery.

To achieve the best results in your embroidery, you should always try to harmonize your material and your pattern.